"The Wicked Borroweth, and Returneth Not Again"

Margaret B. Allen

AN AMBASSADOR'S MEMOIRS

THE CAPTIVE EMPEROR AT TSARSKOIE-SELO
(Photograph lent by M. Pierre Gilliard)

AN AMBASSADOR'S MEMOIRS   *By Maurice Paléologue* (*Last French Ambassador to the Russian Court*)

Translated by F. A. HOLT, O.B.E.

VOL. III
(August 19, 1916—May 17, 1917)

THIRD EDITION

NEW YORK: GEORGE H. DORAN COMPANY

PRINTED IN GREAT BRITAIN

CONTENTS

CHAPTER I

AUGUST 19—SEPTEMBER 18, 1916

AMBASSADOR'S MEMOIRS

Vol. III

CHAPTER I

August 19—September 18, 1916

The Empress's *camarilla* : the direction in which she endeavours to influence Russian diplomacy.—The Salonica army ties down the Bulgarians on the Macedonian front in order to cover the mobilization of the Rumanian army.—The political education of Nicholas II : " The Emperor will always be Pobiedonostzev's pupil ! "—Victories of the Russian army in Upper Armenia.—The Empress and Sturmer ; he treats her as the regent.—Exhaustion of the Russian forces on the Galician front.—One of the Russian regiments sent to France mutinies at Marseilles.—The arrest of Manuilov, director of Sturmer's secretariat.—*Ennui*, the chronic disease of Russian society.—Influence of the Jewish question on relations between Russia and America.—The perilous situation of Rumania ; the action at Turtukai ; invasion of the Dobrudja ; the Russian General Staff studies the possibility of sending an army to help in the Danube region.—The strategic plan of Marshal Hindenburg.—Rasputin and Sturmer ; their conferences in the Fortress of SS. Peter and Paul.—Russian notions of time and space.

Saturday, August 19, 1916.

During the last few days I have had many talks with persons of all shades of opinion. When I sum up all they tell me—and, even more, what they do not tell me—I arrive at the following conclusions.

Without the Emperor's approval or knowledge, the Empress's *camarilla* is endeavouring to influence Russian diplomacy in a new direction, i.e., preparing the ground for a reconciliation with Germany. The predominating motive is fear, the fear to which the reactionary party is inspired on seeing Russia involved in so close and prolonged an association with the democratic powers of the West ; I have referred to this matter several times before.

There is also the community of industrial and commercial
interests which existed before the war between Germany
and Russia and which many are anxious to re-establish.
And again there is the poor result of the recent offensive
of the Russian armies on the Dvina, a result which proves
that the military resistance of Germany is far from being
exhausted. On the other hand, the successes in Galicia
and Armenia have popularized the idea that the profits
of the war must be made at the expense of Austria and
Turkey rather than that of Germany.

* * *

Sunday, August 20, 1916.

The Salonica army, an army of not less than four hundred
thousand men under the command of General Sarrail, is to
take the offensive to-day between the Vardar and the
Struma, north-west of Seres. As provided by Article 3 of
the Bucharest Military Convention, it is an endeavour to
hold down the Bulgarians on the Macedonian front in
order to cover the mobilization and concentration of the
Rumanian army.

* * *

Tuesday, August 22, 1916

The ex-Minister for Agriculture, Krivoshein, who is
undoubtedly the most open-minded and intellectual of the
liberal imperialists, was telling me not long ago of the
stubborn and invincible resistance opposed by the Emperor
to anyone who advises him to allow tsarism to develop
in the direction of parliamentary monarchy. He concluded with the depressing remark :

"The Emperor will always be Pobiedonostzev's
pupil ! "

Who can doubt that it is to the famous procurator of
the Holy Synod, the close friend and colleague of
Alexander III, that Nicholas II owes the whole of his
political and moral education. An eminent jurist and
learned theologian, the fanatical champion of orthodox
autocracy, Pobiedonostzev brought to the advocacy of his

reactionary doctrines ardent conviction, exalted patriotism, a lofty and inflexible conscience, culture of an immense range, rare dialectical skill and lastly—though it seems contradictory—unaffected simplicity and great charm of manner and conversation. His whole programme could be summed up in the words " absolutism, nationalism, orthodoxy," and he pursued its fulfilment with an uncompromising ruthlessness and sovereign scorn of the realities which stood in his path. To him " the modern spirit," democratic principles and western atheism were necessarily anathema. His stubborn, daily influence left an indelible mark on the impressionable mind of Nicholas II.

In 1896, just at the time when he was completing the political education of his young sovereign, Pobiedonostzev published a volume of *Thoughts*. I have just been reading it, and note the following suggestive reflections :

" One of the most erroneous political principles is that of popular sovereignty, the idea—widespread, unfortunately, since the French Revolution—that all power comes from the people and has its source in the national will. The greatest of the evils of the constitutional system is the formation of ministries on the parliamentary pattern, based on the numerical standing of parties. . . . The body and the spirit cannot be separated. The body and the spirit live one, inseparable life. . . . The atheist state is merely a Utopia, for atheism is the negation of the State. Religion is the spiritual force which creates law. That is why the worst enemies of public order never fail to proclaim that religion is a personal, private affair. . . . The ease with which men allow themselves to be deluded by the commonplaces of popular sovereignty and individual liberty leads to general demoralization and the decay of the political sense. France offers us to-day a striking example of that demoralization and decay ; the contagion is already reaching England. . . ."

* * *

Thursday, August 24, 1916.

The general offensive which the Salonica army was preparing to open on August 20 was anticipated on the

18th by an audacious attack by the Bulgarians. Their main effort was made on the two extremities of our line, in the Doiran region east of the Vardar, and Western Macedonia south of Monastir. The Serbians were holding the latter sector and the blow was so violent that they have had to fall back for thirty kilometres, thus losing the towns of Florina and Koritza which the enemy at once occupied. The news has produced great agitation in Bucharest.

* * *

Sunday, August 27, 1916.

The Russian army is developing its operations in Upper Armenia in the most brilliant fashion. It has just occupied Mush, west of Lake Van. The Turks are retreating through Bitlis on Mosul.

* * *

Monday, August 28, 1916.

Italy declared war on Germany yesterday, thus consummating the breach with Germanism ; Rumania has also declared war on Austria-Hungary.

* * *

Tuesday, August 29, 1916.

A former president of the Council, Kokovtsov, is passing through Petrograd and I called on him this afternoon.

I found him more pessimistic than ever. The dismissal of Sazonov and General Bielaiev has made him extremely uneasy.

" The Empress is now all-powerful," he said. " Sturmer is incapable and vain but astute and shrewd enough when his personal interests are at stake, and had known only too well how to make her serve his purposes. He reports regularly to her, tells her everything, consults her on all points, treats her as the regent and trains her in the notion that as the Emperor has received his power from God he has to account for it to God alone, so that it is sacrilege for anyone to take the liberty of opposing the imperial will. You can imagine how much an argument of that kind appeals to the brain of a mystic ! Thus it has come about that Khvostov, Krivoshein, General Polivanov, Samarin, Sazonov, General Bielaiev and myself are now regarded as revolutionaries, traitors and infidels ! "

" Do you think there is no remedy for this state of affairs ? "

" None ! It's a tragical situation."

" ' Tragical ' is rather a strong word, isn't it ? "

" Not at all, take my word for it ! It's a tragical situation. Speaking personally, I'm thankful I'm not a minister now, and have no share of responsibility for the catastrophe which is coming. But as a citizen I weep for my country."

Tears stood in his eyes. To recover himself he paced the full length of his room two or three times. Then he talked about the Emperor, without a trace of bitterness or recrimination, but in a tone of the deepest melancholy.

" The Emperor is judicious, moderate and hard working. As a rule his ideas are very sensible. He has a lofty idea of his functions and the strongest sense of duty. But his education is inadequate and the scale of the problems it is his mission to solve only too frequently exceeds the measure of his intelligence. He does not know men, affairs or life itself. His distrust of himself and others means that he is always suspicious of superiority, and the result is that he can only tolerate nobodies around him. He is also very religious, in a narrow and superstitious way, and this makes him very jealous of his authority, as he receives it from God."

We returned to the subject of the Empress :

" I protest with all my might," he said, " against the infamous rumours that are spread abroad about her relations with Rasputin. She's the noblest and purest of women. But she's an invalid, neurotic and a prey to hallucinations : she'll end up in the frenzy of mysticism and melancholy. I shall never forget the extraordinary things she said to me in September, 1911, when I took the place of the unfortunate Stolypin* as President of the

---

* Assassinated at Kiev on September 14, 1911. He was the brother-in-aw of M. Sazonov.

Council. I was telling her of the difficulties of my task and quoting the example of my predecessor when she cut me short: 'Don't mention that man's name again, Vladimir Nicolaievitch. He died because Providence had decreed that he should disappear that day. So he's finished with: never mention his name again.' She also refused to pray at his coffin and the Emperor did not condescend to appear at the funeral, all because Stolypin, devoted, wholly and utterly devoted, to his sovereigns though he was, had dared to tell them that some slight reforms were necessary in the social edifice!'"

* * *

Wednesday, August 30, 1916.

The Salonica army, by vigorous attacks in the region of the Moglenitza and the Beles *massif*, has at last succeeded in tying the Bulgarians down on the Macedonian front. By thus depriving them of the possibilities of strategic movement towards the north, it has entirely fulfilled its mission, a very difficult mission, which was assigned to it by the military convention of August 17.

* * *

Thursday, August 31, 1916.

The Russian armies are continuing their advance from the Stokhod to the Carpathians, i.e., on a front of three hundred and fifty kilometres.

But their progress is very slow, a fact which is explained by the weariness of the men and the horses, the growing difficulties of communications, the wastage of artillery and the necessity of economizing in ammunition.

Thus Rumania enters the war at the moment when the Russian offensive is petering out.

* * *

Friday, September 1, 1916.

There is great humiliation at General Headquarters and the War Ministry.

The 2nd Russian brigade, which recently arrived in France and was about to embark for Salonica, has mutinied at Marseilles ; the colonel has been murdered and several officers were wounded. To restore order the vigorous intervention of French troops was required. Severe measures of repression have been taken and about twenty men shot.

I cannot help remembering what Sazonov said to me last December when justifying his opposition to Doumer's request : " When the Russian soldier is off his own soil he's worthless ; he goes to pieces at once."

* * *

Saturday, September 2, 1916.

Manuilov, the policeman convict whom Sturmer made the director of his secretariat, has just been arrested : he is said to be guilty of blackmailing a bank, a fact which is proved *a priori*, as swindling is his normal method of money-making and the most ordinary and venial of his crimes.

The incident would not have been worth mentioning if the arrest had not been decided upon by the Minister of the Interior, Alexander Khvostov, and carried out without Sturmer's knowledge. So evidently there is something behind it, something more or less scandalous, which we shall hear about before long.

* * *

Sunday, September 3, 1916.

In Galicia the Russians are advancing on Kalicz.

North of the Transylvanian Alps the Rumanians have captured Brasso. In the region of the Upper (Moldavian) Sereth they are operating side by side with the Russians and crossing the Carpathians.

On the Salonica side the army of General Sarrail is continuing to harass the Bulgarians.

On the Somme the Anglo-French offensive has been resumed with great vigour.

* * *

Monday, September 4, 1916.

At tea time at Madame S——'s house to-day, we were

B

talking about *ennui*, which is the chronic disease of Russian society.

Tall and lithe, the pretty Princess D——, standing with her hands behind her back—her usual posture—was listening to us in silence.   In the depths of her brown eyes there was a glow of scepticism and reverie : suddenly and quite casually she let fall the following remarks :

" It's a funny thing.   When you men are afflicted with *ennui* it knocks you flat, makes you helpless.   You're simply good for nothing and it's an exhausting business to get you going again.   But in the case of women, *ennui* rouses us, whips our senses, makes us want to commit every imaginable futility and folly.   And it's even more difficult to hold us back than to revive you."

The observation is perfectly accurate.   Generally speaking the men get bored through exhaustion or satiety, over-indulgence in pleasure, drink or high play, whereas with the women *ennui* is usually brought on by the monotony of their existence, their insatiable craving for emotional excitement, the secret yearnings of their hearts and their passions.   Hence the depression of the former and the feverishness of the latter.

* * *

Tuesday, September 5, 1916.

I have been talking about America with Neratov.   We both regret that so large a fraction of the American people still refuses to realize the universal significance of the conflict which is devastating Europe, and cannot see which side is in the right.   It is more than a year since a German submarine sank the *Lusitania,* more than a year since the great New York paper, *The Nation,* wrote : " The torpedo-ing of the *Lusitania* is an act which would have made Attila blush, an act of which a Turk would be ashamed and for which a Barbary corsair would have apologized. All human and divine laws have been violated by these bandits . . ."

And still the conscience of America hesitates to declare itself !

I said to Neratov:

" Russia could do a lot to remove the last misgivings of the American public and bring them to our side once and for all."

" What could we do ? I can't imagine."

" All that is necessary is for you to make some slight improvement in your laws dealing with the Jews; the effect in America would be considerable."

Neratov protested:

" What ! Reopen the Jewish question in the middle of a war ! It's impossible. We'd have the whole country against us. That would be an enormous injury to the Alliance; you may be quite sure that our parties of the extreme Right would immediately accuse France and England of having secretly supported the claims of the Jews."

We returned to current topics.

The Jewish question is a heavy cloud over relations between Russia and the United States ; I have often discussed it with my American colleague, Marye, Francis's predecessor.

There are hundreds of thousands of Russian Jews in New York, Chicago, Philadelphia and Boston.* With their energy and intelligence, wealth and influence, they keep hatred of tsarism alive in the United States. The system of persecution which was introduced by Catherine II in 1791, and confirmed and intensified in 1882 by the famous " Ignatiev Laws," is regarded by the Americans as one of the most revolting iniquities which the history of human societies records. I can easily imagine what a free " Yankee," brought up on the superstition of the democratic ideal and the craze and reverence for individual initiative, must think of the idea of five million human beings being confined, on the sole ground of their religious beliefs, to a small area where their very numbers doom them to misery. What must he think of the facts that they

---

* The total number of Jews scattered over the globe is computed to be 12,500,000 ; 5,300,000 in Russia and 2,200,000 in the United States. Outside these two countries the largest Jewish populations are to be found in Austria-Hungary (2,250,000), Germany (615,000), Turkey (485,000), England (445,000), France (345,000), Rumania (260,000), and Holland (115,000).

cannot own or cultivate land, are deprived of all public rights, their slightest acts exposed to the arbitrary control of the police and are always living in fear of periodical massacre ?

My American colleague, Marye, said to me one day :

" What shocks us most about the position of the Jews in Russia is that they are persecuted solely on the ground of their faith. The reproaches of race and economic grievances are only pretexts. This must be so because a Jew has only to abjure judaism and become converted to orthodoxy to be immediately treated like any other Russian."

In 1904 the pogroms at Kishinev aroused such indignation in the United States that President Roosevelt thought it his duty to make a solemn protest, an act which Russian society hotly resents even now : " Crimes are sometimes committed," he declared, " so monstrous that we wonder if it is not our bounden duty to express our detestation of the oppressors and our pity for the victims. Of course we cannot intervene save in very grave cases. But in extreme cases our intervention is legitimate. The American nation owes it to itself to confess its horror when it hears of massacres as terrible as those of Kishinev."

* * *

Thursday, September 7, 1916.

Bratiano's mistake in repudiating the Rudeanu agreement, a mistake shared by his allies when they accepted that repudiation, is beginning to bear fruit.

While the Rumanian troops are advancing beyond the Carpathians and occupying Brasso, Hermannstadt and Orsova, the Austro-Bulgarians are invading the Dobrudja and approaching Silistria. A Rumanian division which was in an exposed position on the right bank of the Danube in the neighbourhood of Turtukai, has just suffered a serious reverse. Surrounded by four Germano-Bulgarian divisions, it has lost twelve thousand men and two hundred guns.

The shock of this news has filled Bucharest with consternation and the agitation is all the greater because the city has been assiduously bombed by hostile aviators for the last three days.

* * *

General Joffre, who is very naturally uneasy about the peril to Rumania, is asking that two hundred thousand Russians shall be sent to the Dobrudja at once.

In conversation with Sturmer I have vigorously seconded his request, pointing out that the whole policy of the Alliance and the very issue of the war are at stake. He replied :

" During my recent visit to Mohilev I considered with General Alexeïev whether it would not be possible to intensify our operations against Bulgaria. The General certainly does not fail to realize what an enormous advantage it would be to us to restore communication with Salonica at the earliest possible moment. But he says that he is without the necessary resources. Of course the problem is not merely how to send two hundred thousand men to the Dobrudja ; it's a question of forming those two hundred thousand men into army corps, with officers, horses, artillery and all the accessory services ; we have no such reserves so they have to be taken from the front. No doubt you know that at the present moment there is no part of our line where fighting is not in progress. General Alexeïev is continuing his operations with the greatest intensity, particularly as the bad weather is coming. So I doubt whether he will agree to suggest to His Majesty the despatch of an army south of the Danube. And don't forget the time it would take to organize and transport that army. Six weeks at least ! Wouldn't it be a grave error to neutralize two hundred thousand men in that way for so long ? "

" What about the Emperor ? Have you mentioned it to him ? "

" The Emperor quite agrees with General Alexeïev."

" The matter is serious enough to deserve further consideration. So please be good enough to refer to His Majesty again and acquaint him with my arguments."

" I'll report our conversation to His Majesty to-day."

Saturday, September 9, 1916.

A Russian financier, of Danish origin, who is in constant business touch with Sweden and, through that channel, always well informed about public opinion in Germany, said to me to-day :

"In the last few weeks Germany has been suffering generally from an attack of war-weariness and apprehension. No one now believes in the sudden overwhelming victory which will bring a victorious peace. Only the uncompromising Pan-Germans still affect to believe in it. The invincible resistance of the French at Verdun and the Russian advance in Galicia have produced a deep sense of disappointment which is not diminishing. People are also beginning to say that the submarine war is a stupid mistake, that it in no way prevents France and England from obtaining supplies, that the Teutonic Powers are faced with the danger of seeing the United States declare war on them before long, etc. Lastly economic discomforts are on the increase and there are frequent strikes, particularly in northern Germany, due to food restrictions. With a view to combating this wave of pessimism the Kaiser has just made Marshal von Hindenburg Chief of the General Staff in General von Falkenhayn's place. The appointment has restored the spirits of the public somewhat. All the hopes of the German people are now centred in the saviour of East Prussia, the victor of Tannenberg. The official press is lavish with dithyrambs exalting the nobility of his character, the grandeur of his ideas and the genius of his strategy ; it does not fear to call him the equal of Moltke, and to compare him to the great Frederick. It is assumed that he will want to justify this enthusiastic confidence at the earliest possible moment. As, for the time being, no victory is possible on the Russian or western fronts, it is presumed that he will seek his triumph in Rumania.

* *

Tuesday, September 12, 1916.

Princess Paley invited me to dinner this evening with the Grand Duchess Marie Pavlovna.

It was a very private party, and I was particularly glad to have a talk with the Grand Duchess as I had not seen her since Sazonov's dismissal.

We continued our conversation from the point at which we left off and took stock of all the changes. Our information was identical : the Empress is taking an ever growing part in politics and the Emperor is offering an ever diminishing resistance to her.

" For example," said the Grand Duchess, " the Emperor loathes Sturmer ; he knows he's incapable and dishonest ; he sees through all his advances to the Empress and is uneasy about it, as he's as jealous of his authority with the Empress as with anyone else. But he had not the courage to uphold Sazonov and he let Sturmer be thrust upon him."

" Isn't there anyone in his household who can open his eyes ? "

" No one. You know the crowd around him. Old Fredericks is still the only person who can talk really frankly to him. But he hasn't any influence. In any case, you must not think that the Emperor's eyes need opening all that much. He knows quite well what he's doing ; he fully realizes his mistakes and faults. His judgment is almost always sound. I'm sure that at the present moment he's extremely sorry he ever got rid of Sazonov."

" Then why does he go on making all these mistakes ? After all, the consequences fall directly on his own head."

" Because he's weak. He hasn't the energy to face the Empress's brow-beating, much less the scenes she makes ! And there's another reason which is far more serious : he's a fatalist. When things are going badly he tells himself it is God's will and he must bow to it ! I've seen him in this state of mind before, after the disasters in Manchuria and during the 1905 troubles."

" But is he in that frame of mind at the present moment ? "

" I'm afraid he's not far from it ; I know he's dejected, and worried to find the war going on so long without any result."

" Do you think he's capable of abandoning the struggle and making peace ? "

" No, never ; at any rate, not so long as there's an enemy soldier on Russian soil. He took that oath in the sight of God and he knows that if he broke it his eternal salvation would be jeopardized. And then he has a lofty conception of honour and will not betray his allies ; he will be unshakable on that point. I believe I told you before that he would go to his death rather than sign a shameful or treacherous peace."

* * *

Wednesday, September 13, 1916.

General Janin has reported to me a conversation he had with the Emperor yesterday at Mohilev, a conversation which unfortunately confirms what Sturmer said to me five days ago.

The Emperor has told him that he is not in a position to send two hundred thousand men to the Dobrudja, on the ground that the armies in Galicia and Asia have suffered very heavy losses during the last few weeks and he is obliged to send them all the available reinforcements. As he ended he asked General Janin to telegraph to General Joffre and say that he urgently begs him to order General Sarrail to act with greater energy. The Emperor repeated : " It's a personal request from me to General Joffre."

* * *

Thursday, September 14, 1916.

For some time there has been a rumour that Rasputin and Sturmer have fallen out : they are never met together, they never call on each other. And yet they see and consult each other daily. Their meetings take place in the evening in the Fortress of SS. Peter and Paul, the most secret place in Petrograd.

The Governor of the Romanov Bastille is General Nitikin, whose daughter is one of the most fervent adorers of the *staretz*. It is through her that messages pass between Sturmer and Grishka ; she it is who goes to find

Rasputin in the town and brings him in her carriage to the fortress ; it is in the Governor's house, in fact Mlle. Nitikin's own room, that the two accomplices hold conclave.

Why do they wrap themselves up in so much mystery ? Why have they selected this secret hiding-place ? Why do they only meet at night ? May it be that they know that everyone loathes them and they wish to conceal the closeness of their association from the public ? Perhaps, too, they fear that the bomb of some anarchist may disturb their meetings.

Of all the tragic spectacles which have left memories in this fearsome state prison, are there any more sinister than the nocturnal gatherings of these two criminals who are ruining Russia ?

* * *

Friday, September 15, 1916.

In this diary I have frequently had occasion to remark that the Russians have no precise ideas of *space* and usually content themselves with vague estimates and approximate figures. Their notion of *time* is just as vague. I was struck by this fact once more to-day at an administrative conference in Sturmer's house in which methods of assisting Rumania were under examination. In the transport programme presented to us most of the dates were uncertain, the intervals too short or too long, the timings problematical. Of course this inability to realize the temporal relations of facts is still more obvious in the case of the illiterate, who are the mass. The whole economic life of the Russian nation is kept back by it.

The phenomenon is explained easily enough if it be admitted that the accurate visualization of time is simply an order of succession introduced into our memories and plans, an organization of our mental ideas with reference to a focussing-point which is our present state. With the Russians that focussing-point is usually shifting or misty, because their perception of reality is never very distinct, they do not clearly define their sensations and notions, their power of attention is low and their reasoning

and calculations are almost always blended with the
imaginary.

* * *

Saturday, September 16, 1916.

Under the increasing pressure of the Bulgarians the
Rumanians are progressively evacuating the Dobrudja,
and every day and night Austrian airmen bomb Bucharest
from their base at Rustchuk.

From the moment the Rudeanu agreement was thrown
over these misfortunes were easy to foresee. The Rumanian
Government is paying dearly for the mistake it made in
directing its whole military effort towards Transylvania,
allowing itself to be taken in by vague rumours from
Sofia and particularly in imagining that the Bulgarians
had abandoned the idea of a military revenge for the
disaster and humiliation of 1913.

* * *

Sunday, September 17, 1916.

Sylvia and *The Water-Lily* were given at the Marie
Theatre this evening. In both works the lead is in the
hands of Karsavina.

The sumptuous hall, with its blue and gold hangings,
was quite full; the evening marked the opening of the
winter season and the resumption of those ballets in which
the Russian imagination loves to follow the interplay of
flying forms and rhythmic movements through the music.
From the stalls to the back row of the highest circle I
could see nothing but a sea of cheery, smiling faces. In
the intervals the boxes came to life with the irresponsible
chatter which made the bright eyes of the women sparkle
with merriment. Irksome thoughts of the present,
sinister visions of war and the melancholy prospects of
the future vanished as if by magic the moment the
orchestra struck up. An air of pleasant unreality was in
every face.

Thomas de Quincy, the author of the *Confessions of an
Opium Eater*, tells us that the drug often gave him the

illusions of music. Conversely, the Russians go to music for the effects of opium.

* * *

Monday, September 18, 1916.

The Salonica army has resumed the offensive on the whole of the Macedonian front. The Bulgarians have been driven back in the neighbourhood of Florina and are now withdrawing towards Monastir

CHAPTER II

SEPTEMBER 19—OCTOBER 25, 1916

CHAPTER II

SEPTEMBER 19—OCTOBER 25, 1916

The heralds of winter.—The Church of the Saviour-on-the-Waters.—The Emperor is often charged with being heartless.—The combined effort of the Allies to relieve Rumania.—Public education in Russia: the primary schools.—Ignorance of the rural masses; a contrast with the brilliant development of science, letters and art.—A political crisis in Athens; Venizelos goes to Crete.—Prince Kanin's visits to Petrograd: the reflections of a *moujik*.—Another Minister of the Interior: Protopopov; his relations with Rasputin.—Sturmer's treachery; the intrigues of which he is the centre.—Clandestine activities of the socialist leaders.—Successive defeats of the Rumanian army; a very grave situation.—General Berthelot passes through Petrograd on his way to take command of the French mission in Rumania.—My Japanese colleague, Viscount Motono, is appointed Minister for Foreign Affairs; a great authority on Asiatic and European problems.— The Minister of Communications, Trepov, boldly attacks Sturmer; his confidence in the Emperor.—German agents in Petrograd: dinners at the house of Manus, the financier.—Costanza captured by the Austro-Bulgarians; the Rumanians evacuate the Dobrudja.

Tuesday, September 19, 1916.

Winter is already at hand. Under the livid sky a slow-falling, invisible and icy rain seems to fill the air with a snowy vapour. The light is going by four o'clock. I was finishing my drive about that hour and happened to pass the little church of the Saviour-on-the-Waters which is on the bank of the Neva, near the Arsenal. I stopped my carriage and got out to visit this poetic sanctuary which I have not entered since the war.

It is one of the very few churches in Petrograd in which the conventional and showy style of Italo-Germanic architecture has not had its fling; it is perhaps the only one in which the worshipper breathes an atmosphere of quiet meditation and an odour of mysticism. It was built in 1910 in memory of the twelve thousand sailors who died in the war against Japan, and is an exquisite copy of Muscovite art in the twelfth century, the church of Bogoliubovo, near Vladimir.

Externally it has simple, well-defined lines, with Roman arches and a graceful dome. In the warm half-darkness inside, the sole decoration of the bare walls consists of bronze plaques on which are engraved the names of all the vessels, officers and men lost at Port Arthur, Vladivostock and Tsushima. I know nothing more moving in its very simplicity than this memorial church. But one's feelings are transformed and touch on the sublime at the sight of the iconostasis. In the depths of the dark apse a figure of Christ, more than life size, hovers and glows in a golden cloud above black waves. In the majesty of the attitude, the nobility of the gestures and the infinite pity which speaks in the eyes, this figure reminds one of the finest Byzantine mosaics.

When I first visited this church, at the beginning of 1914, I did not realize all the pathetic symbolism of this sacred figure. To-day its grandeur and eloquence seemed prodigious, as if it were an interpretation of that last vision which has soothed and sanctified the dying moments of thousands upon thousands during this war.

By a natural connection of ideas I remembered what Rasputin said to the Empress one day when she was weeping on hearing of the enormous losses in a great battle: " Take heart! When a *moujik* dies for his Tsar and country, another lamp is immediately lit before the throne of God."

* * *

Wednesday, September 20, 1916.

Hindenburg's plan is taking shape and in course of realization on the whole of the circular Rumanian front. Along the Danube and in the Dobrudja the region of Orsova and the defiles of the Carpathians, the German, Austrian, Bulgarian and Turkish forces are exercising sustained and converging pressure, under which the Rumanians are giving way at all points.

* * *

Thursday, September 21, 1916.

I often hear the Emperor accused of heartlessness and

selfishness. He is charged with having always shown himself indifferent not only to the misfortunes of his relatives, friends and most faithful servants, but even to the sorrows of his people. Several memorable incidents are quoted in which he certainly displayed astonishing indifference.

The first occasion was during the celebrations attending his coronation at Moscow on May 18, 1896. A public fête had been arranged in Khodinsky meadow, near Petrovsky park. But the police arrangements were so bad that the crowd began to heave violently. Suddenly there seemed to be a panic and a general stampede ensued ; there were four thousand victims, of which two thousand died. When Nicholas II heard of the catastrophe he did not display the slightest sign of emotion and did not even cancel a ball for that evening.

Nine years later, on May 14, 1905, Admiral Rojdest-vensky's fleet was utterly destroyed ; with it disappeared Russia's whole future in the Far East. The Emperor was just about to play a game of tennis when the telegram announcing the disaster was handed to him. He simply said : " What a horrible catastrophe ! " and without another word, asked for his racket.

It was with the same unruffled composure that he received the news of the assassination of the Minister of the Interior, Plehve, in 1904, of his uncle, the Grand Duke Sergei, in 1905, and of Stolypin, his President of the Council, in 1911.

And, quite recently, the hasty, underhand way in which he dismissed his close associate, Prince Orlov, has again revealed a stratum of callousness in him, a soul all but impervious to the generous impulses of gratitude and friendship.

After referring to all these incidents, old Princess D——, who has known the Emperor since his childhood, concluded with the bitter remark :

" Nicholas Alexandrovitch has no heart at all."

I protested that for all that, he appears to be capable of affection towards his own family ; he is certainly extremely devoted to the Empress ; he adores his daughters

c

and idolizes his son. He cannot be denied instincts of tenderness. I am inclined to think that the superhuman situation in which he is placed has gradually changed his feelings towards other men and that his indifference is also one result of his fatalism

* * *

Friday, September 22, 1916.

Are Sturmer's political fortunes in danger ? I am told that, judging by credible indications, his bitter enemy, the Minister of the Interior, Khvostov, has turned the Emperor completely against him by telling His Majesty the inner history of the Manuilov affair and making him extremely alarmed at the prospect of an imminent scandal. What is this inner history ? We do not know ; but it cannot be doubted that there are one or more corpses between Sturmer and the director of his secretariat.

It is even being said that the question of Sturmer's successor as President of the Council has already been settled in secret. The choice is said to have fallen on the present Minister of Communications, Alexander Feodoro-vitch Trepov. I could only congratulate myself on such an appointment. Trepov is as honest, intelligent and hard-working as energetic and patriotic.

I dined this evening at the Donon restaurant with Kokovtsov and Putilov. The ex-President of the Council and the millionaire banker outbid each other with lugubrious forebodings.

Kokovtsov said :

" We're heading for revolution."

Putilov added :

" We're heading for anarchy."

To explain himself, he continued :

" The Russian is not a revolutionary ; he's an anarchist. There's a world of difference. The revolutionary means to reconstruct ; the anarchist thinks only of destroying."

Saturday, September 23, 1916.

The Allies are attacking on all the fronts with a view to taking the weight off Rumania.

In Artois and Picardy the English and French have carried an extensive series of German trenches by storm. In the Isonzo region the Italians are intensifying their offensive east of Gorizia. In Macedonia the English are crossing the Struma whilst the French and Serbians, after occupying Florina, are hustling the Bulgarians in the direction of Monastir. In Volhynia the Russians are harassing the Austro-Germans from the Pinsk marshes to Lutzk. In Galicia they are advancing on Lemberg and south-west of Kalicz. In the Bukovina Carpathians they have captured several hostile positions north of Dorma Vatra.

* * *

Sunday, September 24, 1916.

A popular misconception, both in France and England (and I am always hearing the echo of it) is that tsarism would easily settle its domestic difficulties if it abandoned its antiquated principles and boldly entered the path of democratic reforms. It is said that all the latent energies and unsuspected virtues of the Russian people would be revealed at once. There would be a prodigious outpouring of patriotism, intelligence, moral fervour, force of character, spirit of initiative and organization, practical idealism, lofty conceptions of social, national and human duty. The western Allies should therefore put pressure on the Emperor Nicholas to make him adopt the necessary innovations. The change would also mean doubling the effective power of the Alliance.

The recent visit of the " Cadet " deputies to London and Paris has contributed not a little to the spread of these ideas. These gentlemen have even made a complaint about myself—the complaint that I am not seen enough in liberal circles, that I do not display my sympathy with them as openly as I might and do not take advantage of my friendly relations with the Emperor to convert him to parliamentary principles.

In this diary I have on several occasions explained the attitude of reserve I have felt bound to adopt towards the liberal parties. Whatever the defects of tsarism may be, it is the tie-beam of Russia, the basis and framework of Russian society, the sole link between the heterogeneous territories and peoples which ten centuries of history have gradually gathered under the sceptre of the Romanovs. So long as the war lasts the Allies must therefore uphold it at any cost. I have frequently developed this argument.

But I go further : I am convinced that for a long time to come, one or two generations perhaps, the internal evils from which Russia is suffering will only admit of treatment which is palliative, partial and cautiously graduated. The outstanding reason is the colossal ignorance in which the mass of the Russian nation is vegetating.

It is there that the real weakness of Russia lies, and the principal source of her incapacity for political progress can be found. In this vast empire there are not more than one hundred and twenty thousand primary schools for a population of one hundred and eighty million souls. And *such* schools, *such* teachers ! As a general rule the teaching is entrusted to the parish priest who is usually a poor creature, idle and despised. In his syllabus reading, writing and arithmetic take second place to prayers, the catechism, sacred history and church music. Thus the education of the nation is more or less directly in the hands of the clergy. The Holy Synod recently reminded its priests that the schools must be kept " in the closest association with the church, and in strict observance of the orthodox faith," and that the religious education of the children must be " the first concern of the masters."

The system functions in the most defective manner. In many districts the schools are poorly attended or actually empty, either because of the distances, snow and cold, or because educational material and books are lacking, or the *moujiks* have quarrelled with the priest and thrashed him too hard.

To the great Catherine, the empress-philosopher and friend of Voltaire and Diderot, is due the credit, as of so much else, of founding public education in Russia. Some twenty secondary schools and a hundred primary schools were established in her reign. She threw herself into this enterprise with her usual enthusiasm, though without forgetting those principles of government which still inspire her successors. One day, when the governor of Moscow was complaining of the indifference his citizens displayed towards the new institution, the tsarina replied : "Are you complaining because the Russians don't try to educate themselves ? I didn't start these schools for *their* sake, but for the sake of Europe, where we must keep our place in public opinion. If a day comes when our peasants want to be educated, neither you nor I will remain where we are."

* * *

Monday, September 25, 1916.

Thinking over what I wrote yesterday about the general ignorance of the Russian nation, it is a pleasure by contrast to draw up a list of all the eminent men who are the glory of Russia to-day in the domain of science, thought, literature and art ; for if the masses are un-educated and backward, the élite are brilliant, active, highly productive and vigorous. I know few countries which can produce so fine a contingent of great minds, unprejudiced, luminous and discerning intellects, original, fascinating and irrepressible talent.

There is fierce rivalry in all the departments of scientific work. Nowhere is experimental and practical science more worthily represented, as it is carried on by biologists such as Pavlov and Metchnikov, chemists such as Mendeleïev, physicists like Lebedev, geologists like Karpinsky and mathematicians like Liapunov, Vassiliev and Krylov ; I will even venture the opinion that Pavlov and Mendeleïev are as great as Claude Bernard and Lavoisier.

The historians, archæologists and ethnographers also form a solid phalanx of erudite and sagacious investigators. I need only name Kliutchevsky, Miliukov, Platonov and Rostovtsev in the historical field ; in the archæological, Vesselovsky and Kondakov ; in the ethnographical, Moguilansky. Several groups of linguists have been doing excellent work for many years, displaying the same strict method and the same subtle power of analysis and intuition. Professors Chakmohtov and Zelinsky are up to the level of the best foreign masters.

Philosophy has never been highly developed in the empire of the Tsars, any more than it could develop in the Papal states in the days of temporal power : when theological dogmatism has a society in its grip philosophers necessarily feel themselves hampered. On the other hand, metaphysical speculation is seriously cultivated in intellectual circles in Petrograd and Moscow ; its leading experts are Lopatin, Berdiaev and Prince Sergei Trubetzkoi, the disciple and successor of the great idealist, Vladimir Soloviev.

Imaginative literature, though still mourning the loss of Tolstoi and Dostoievsky, displays a vitality in every branch which justifies the greatest hopes. From the generous output of these last ten years one could extract some thirty works, novels or plays, which are remarkable for their chaste beauty of form, careful composition, regard for moral and pictorial truth, psychological divination, the lifelike quality of the characters, the corroding flavour of pessimism, the vivid portrayal of life, turbid or sordid, insatiable or passive, the moving obsession of mental derangement, and last but not least the clear and tragic vision of social problems. Several writers who have thus made their mark since 1905 have already disappeared ; but to judge the evolution of the literary movement in Russia, an assembly of talents so varied as those of Gorky, Anreiev, Korolenko, Veressaiev, Merejovsky, Madame Hippius, Artzibachev, Kuprin, Kamensky, Sologub, Kuzmin, Ivanov, Bunin, Tchirykov, Gumilov and Brussov certainly constitutes one of the most favourable symptoms.

There is the same vitality in painting, in which realistic and national tendencies are sometimes so happily brought out under the brush of Repin, Golovin, Roerich, Somov, Maliavin, and Vrubel, not to mention the powerful portrait-painter Serov, who died four years ago. And could I omit the names of the two men responsible for the revolution in theatrical decoration, those marvellous magicians of scenic illusion, Alexander Benois and Bakst ?

In music the glorious era of Balakirev, Moussorgsky Borodin and Rimsky-Korsakov is over. But their artistic offspring, Glazunov, Scriabin, Stravinsky, Rachmaninov and young Prokofiev, are manfully continuing the great tradition and as anxious to prolong it as to enrich and extend it. With the wealth and freedom of its inspiration, the dreamy and enticing grace of the melodic design, its fertility of invention, the brilliance of orchestral colour and the bold pursuit of polyphonic complexities, Russian music seems to be on the very threshold of a second blooming.

* * *

Tuesday, September 26, 1916.

The situation in Athens is getting worse : the duel between the King and Venizelos has reached the critical phase.

A Russian journalist, who to my knowledge has some kind of relations with Sturmer, has just been to see me to tell me privately that " certain people at court " are not at all sorry to contemplate the possibility of a dynastic crisis in Greece, and are even cherishing hopes that the French will precipitate that crisis, " which would be so advantageous to the cause of the Allies."

I cautiously replied that the views which inspire Briand's policy towards Greece in no way involve a dynastic crisis and that it is for King Constantine himself to carry out the splendid programme of national expansion which the Allies have put before him.

He dropped the subject.

It is quite easy to see through the designs of Sturmer and the " people at court." Obviously the disciples of Russian autocracy could not be a party to overturning a throne. But if events in Greece are bound to lead to the proclamation of a republic, would it not be better, they say, to put a swift stop to the crisis by a change of monarch ? There is no lack of candidates in the Russian imperial family. And as an autocratic government could not decently undertake so dirty a job as the dethronement of a King, does not everything show that the government of the French Republic is designated for this operation ?

Prince Kotohito Kanin, cousin of the Mikado, is arriving in Petrograd to-morrow ; he has come to return the visit which the Grand Duke George Michailovitch recently paid to the Emperor Yoshihito.

On orders from the police, bunches of Russian and Japanese flags are being displayed in the streets.

These preparations are prompting the *moujiks* to curious reflections. My naval attaché, Commander Gallaud, has been telling me that when he was driving in the Champ-de-Mars to-day, his *isvostchik* turned round, pointed to some recruits who were drilling and asked him in a sly tone :

" What are they being drilled for ? "

" To fight the Germans."

" What's the good ? Look at me. I was in the Manchurian campaign myself in 1905 ; I was wounded at Mukden. And now ! Look at them hanging out flags from all the houses and raising triumphal arches on the Nevsky Prospekt in honour of this Japanese prince who is coming ! In a few years it'll be the same with the Germans. We shall be welcoming *them* under triumphal arches. Then why have thousands and thousands of men killed if all this is bound to end like the Japanese business?"

* * *

Wednesday, September 27, 1916.

Sturmer has just spent three days with the Emperor at Mohilev.

I am told that he put his case with great skill. He has come out of the Manuilov affair as well as he could hope, pleading that if he erred it was only through innocence and too much kindness of heart. He emphasized the point that the Duma is shortly to meet, there is a ferment of revolutionary feeling and that it is more vital than ever not to weaken the government. But all his eloquence would have been wasted if the Empress had not supported him with all her stubborn energy. He has been saved.

I saw him in his room to-day; he looked pleased and confident. I asked him about military matters first.

" Does General Alexeïev fully realize the great, the vital importance to the common cause, of the safety of Rumania ? "

" I have been able to satisfy myself that General Alexeïev attaches very high importance to the operations in the Dobrudja. Four Russian divisions and one Serbian division have already crossed the Danube; another Serbian division will be sent there shortly. But that is the most that His Majesty has authorized him to do in that quarter. You know that we have to cope with enormous forces in the region of Kovel and Stanislau."

He confirmed a fact which my officers had already mentioned to me—that the Russian armies in Galicia have recently suffered excessive losses without any appreciable result. Between Pinsk and the Carpathians they are fighting twenty-nine German divisions, forty Austro-Hungarian and two Turkish; their task is made extremely difficult by their inadequate supply of heavy artillery and aeroplanes.

Then we discussed the ministerial crisis which is at hand in Athens and the nationalist movement of which Venizelos is the centre.

" I've not yet had time," said Sturmer, " to read all the telegrams that have arrived to-night but I can tell you *now* that the Emperor has used very stern language about King Constantine."

* * *

Thursday, September 28, 1916.

Bombshell in Greece. Venizelos and Admiral Condouriotis have secretly sailed for Crete where the insurgents have declared in favour of the Entente; nationalist demonstrators are parading the streets of Athens and thousands of officers and men are gathering at the Piræus, demanding to be sent to Salonica so that they can take service in General Sarrail's army.

I have been considering the possible consequences of these occurrences with Sturmer.

" It's in our own hands whether the situation turns to our advantage," I said, " provided we act promptly and vigorously."

" Yes, yes. Certainly."

Then he hesitatingly remarked, as if picking his words :

" What are we to do if King Constantine persists in his resistance ? "

He gave me a curious look, fixing a questioning and shifty eye upon me. I pretended to be thinking. He repeated his question.

" What are we to do with King Constantine ? "

If his question was not an insinuation it was certainly a bait, and was obviously connected with the pseudo-secret of the Russian journalist.

I replied in evasive terms that I was not yet sufficiently acquainted with the course of events in Athens to venture to offer any practical advice, and added :

" In any case I'd rather wait until Monsieur Briand lets me know his views ; but I won't fail to tell him that in your opinion the position of King Constantine is directly involved in the present crisis."

We then turned to other topics : Prince Kanin's visit and the unfortunate development of the military operations in the Dobrudja and the Transylvanian Alps, etc.

As I was leaving I noticed on the walls of the room three engravings which were not there yesterday. The first was of the Congress of Vienna, the second of the Congress of Paris and the third of the Congress of Berlin.

" I see you like to have inspiring pictures around you, President."

" Yes, you know how passionately fond of history I am. I know nothing more instructive."

" And more deceptive."

" Come, don't be sceptical ! Nobody believes enough ! But you haven't noticed the most interesting thing."

" What's that ? "

" That vacant place ! "

" Well ? "

" That's the place I'm keeping for the picture of the next congress ; it's to be called the Congress of Moscow, if God wills ! "

He crossed himself and closed his eyes a moment, as if breathing a short prayer.

I answered quietly : " But will there be any congress ? Haven't we agreed to make Germany accept our terms ? "

With an ecstatic expression he developed his idea and repeated :

" How splendid it would be at Moscow ! How splendid ! May God grant it ! May God grant it ! "

He was already imagining himself Chancellor of the Empire, the successor of Nesselrode and Gortchakov, opening the general peace congress in the Kremlin. All the pettiness, stupidity and infatuation of the man were laid bare at that moment. All he can see in his heavy task, one of the heaviest ever laid on human shoulders, is an opportunity for bragging——and personal advancement.

This evening I returned, in full uniform, to the Foreign Office, where the President of the Council has given an official banquet to Prince Kanin.

Too much glare, silver and plate, food and music ; too many flowers and servants ! It was all dazzle and noise. I could not help thinking what a better tone there was in Sazonov's time, when official show was still in good taste.

At the head of the table sat the Grand Duke George Michailovitch ; I was on Sturmer's left.

During the whole of dinner we simply talked commonplaces. But at dessert Sturmer said to me *ex abrupto*.

" The Congress of Moscow ! Don't you think it would be a magnificent consecration of the Franco-Russian alliance ? A century after the burning of our sacred city it would see Russia and France proclaiming the peace of the world ! "

He complacently expatiated on this theme.

I continued : " I have no idea of the views of my government as to the seat of the next congress and I should be surprised if, in the present stage of our military operations, Monsieur Briand had even turned his thoughts to so distant an eventuality. In any case, as I told you this morning, I hope there will be no congress. In my opinion it is of great importance for the Allies to agree upon all the general terms of the peace, so that we can make our enemies accept them *en bloc*. Part of the work has already been done ; we are agreed about Constantinople, the Straits, Asia Minor, Transylvania, the Adriatic littoral, etc. The rest will be settled when a favourable opportunity presents itself. But first and foremost we must concentrate on victory. Our motto must be : *Primum et ante omnia, vincere!* Your health, my dear President ! "

During the evening I had a talk with Prince Kanin. He told me of his long residence in France, at the school at Saumur, and then said how much he had been touched by the Emperor's cordial welcome, and what a pleasant impression his reception by the crowd had made upon him. We talked about the war and I noticed how he avoided all detailed discussion and expressed no opinion on situations and facts. Under his cold compliments I could guess his contempt for the vanquished of 1905 who have learned their lesson so badly.

* * *

Friday, September 29, 1916.

The economic situation has become much worse in the last few weeks. The increased cost of living is causing hardship all round. The price of the most elementary necessaries is three times what it was at the beginning of the war ; in the case of wood and eggs it is four times, and in that of butter and soap five times. The main causes of this situation are unfortunately as fundamental as obvious—the closing of foreign markets, congestion on the railways and confusion and dishonesty in the public services.

What will it be in a few weeks' time when we have to cope with the rigours of winter and the tortures of the cold, which are even more cruel than those of hunger ?

Saturday, September 30, 1916.

A stubborn struggle is in progress in Galicia, between the Styr and the Zlota Lipa. The Russians, who have taken the offensive, are trying to force their way through in the region of Krasnie and Brzezany, fifty kilometres from Lemberg.

* * *

Sunday, October 1, 1916.

There has been a reception at the Japanese embassy in honour of Prince Kanin. It has been a particularly brilliant function, the guests including the Grand Duke George, the Grand Duke Sergei, the Grand Duke Cyril, etc.

I congratulated my colleague, Motono, on his success. In his shrewd, phlegmatic way he replied :

" Yes, it's gone off quite well. When I first came as ambassador to Petrograd in 1908, hardly anyone spoke to me ; no one ever asked me out and the Grand Dukes affected not to see me. All that has changed. I have achieved the object I set before me : Japan and Russia are linked by the ties of real friendship."

In the throng around the buffet I spied E——, a high official at court, who has taken a liking to me and never misses an opportunity of pouring his suspicious and extravagant nationalism into my ear. I asked him his news.

Without appearing to have heard my question, he pointed to Sturmer who was holding forth a few feet away from us. Then, with a tragic glare, E—— burst out :

" Why haven't you and your English colleague put a stop to that man's treachery before now, Ambassador ? "

I calmed him down :

" It's a subject I'd like to discuss with you . . . but not here. Come and lunch with me alone on Thursday."

" I'll certainly be there."

* * *

Monday, October 2, 1916.

The battle which has begun between the Styr and the

Zlota Lipa is taking a favourable turn for the Russians, who have pierced the enemy's forward lines and made five thousand prisoners.

But there are indications of a formidable counter-attack by the Germans in the region of Lutzk, a hundred kilometres north.

* * *

Tuesday, October 3, 1916.

Sturmer has succeeded in ruining his mortal enemy, Alexander Khvostov, the Minister of the Interior. Henceforth the Manuilov affair has no terrors for him.

The new Minister of the Interior is one of the vice-presidents of the Duma, Protopopov. Hitherto the Emperor has very seldom chosen his members from the representative chamber. But the selection of Protopopov does not herald any evolution in the direction of parliamentary government. Quite the contrary.

On the strength of his earlier opinions, Protopopov ranked as an " Octobrist," i.e. a very moderate liberal. Last June he was a member of the parliamentary delegation which visited the West ; both in London and Paris he showed himself to be a fervent advocate of the war *à outrance*. But during a short stay in Stockholm on his way back he had a strange conversation with a German agent, Warburg, and though the affair remains somewhat obscure, there is no doubt that he spoke in favour of peace.

When he returned to Petrograd he made common cause with Sturmer and Rasputin, who immediately put him in touch with the Empress. He was soon taken into favour and at once initiated into the secret conclaves at Tsarskoïe-Selo. He was entitled to a place there on the strength of his proficiency in the occult sciences, principally spiritualism, the highest and most doubtful of them all. I also know for certain that he once had an infectious disease which has left him with nervous disorders, and that recently the preliminary symptoms of general paralysis have been observed in him. So the internal policy of the empire is in good hands !

Wednesday, October 4, 1916.

It is the Grand Duke Paul's birthday to-day, and he invited me to dinner with the Grand Duke Cyril and his wife the Grand Duchess Victoria, the Grand Duke Boris, the Grand Duchess Marie Pavlovna, Madame Narishkin, Countess Kreutz, Dimitry Benckendorff, Savinsky and others.

Everyone looked very downcast, and indeed one would have to be blind not to see the portents of disaster which are gathering on the horizon.

The Grand Duchess spoke to me in a voice of anguish about her sister, the Queen of Rumania. I dared not reassure her, for if the Rumanians are still holding their ground in the Carpathians it is only with the greatest difficulty, and if they relax their efforts in the slightest there will be a complete disaster.

" For Heaven's sake, *insist* that reinforcements shall be sent there at once," she said. " From what my poor sister says—and you know how brave she is—there's not a moment to lose. If help is not sent to Rumania without delay, a catastrophe is inevitable."

I told her of my daily protests to Sturmer.

" Theoretically, he agrees to all I say and consents to everything I ask. But in practice he shelters behind General Alexeïev, who does not seem to realize the dangers of the situation. And the Emperor only looks at things through General Alexeïev's eyes."

" The Emperor is in a deplorable frame of mind ! "

Without further explanation, she suddenly rose and, on the excuse of getting a cigarette, rejoined the group of ladies.

I then tackled the Grand Duke Paul, the Grand Duke Boris and the Grand Duke Cyril—one by one. They have seen the Tsar recently ; they move in his circle so that they are well qualified to give me news. But I was very careful not to make my questions too direct, as I knew they would evade them. I introduced the monarch's opinions incidentally and as if not attaching any importance to them ; I referred casually to certain of his decisions or some remark he has made to me. They answered quite candidly.

Their replies, which they could not have concocted together, have left me in no doubt as to the Emperor's moral condition. There has been no change in what he says ; he still proclaims his determination to win and his absolute confidence in victory. But despondency, apathy and resignation can be seen in his actions, appearance, attitude and all the manifestations of the inner man.

* * *

Thursday, October 5, 1916.

E——, the high court functionary, came to lunch at the embassy. To make him quite at home I had not invited any other guests.

As long as we were at table he kept a check on himself because of the servants. When we returned to the drawing-room he tossed down two glasses of brandy, filled a third, lit a cigar and with a flaming countenance looked me full in the face and asked me bluntly.

" Ambassador, why are you and your English colleague waiting to put an end to Monsieur Sturmer's treacheries ? "

" We're waiting until we have some definite grievance against him. Officially we have nothing to complain about ; all his words and actions are all that they ought to be. He's always telling us : ' War to the knife ! No mercy for Germany ! ' As regards his real views and secret manœuvres, we have only impressions and intuitions which carry us no further than conjectures and suspicions. You would be doing us a very great service if you could produce one actual fact to support your beliefs."

" I don't know of any actual fact. But the treachery is obvious enough. Don't you see it ? "

" It's not enough to see it ; I must be in a position to make my Government see it, and then the Emperor. One can't embark on a serious matter like this without even a vestige of evidence."

" You're right."

" As we're reduced to hypotheses for the time being,